WEAR
L O V E

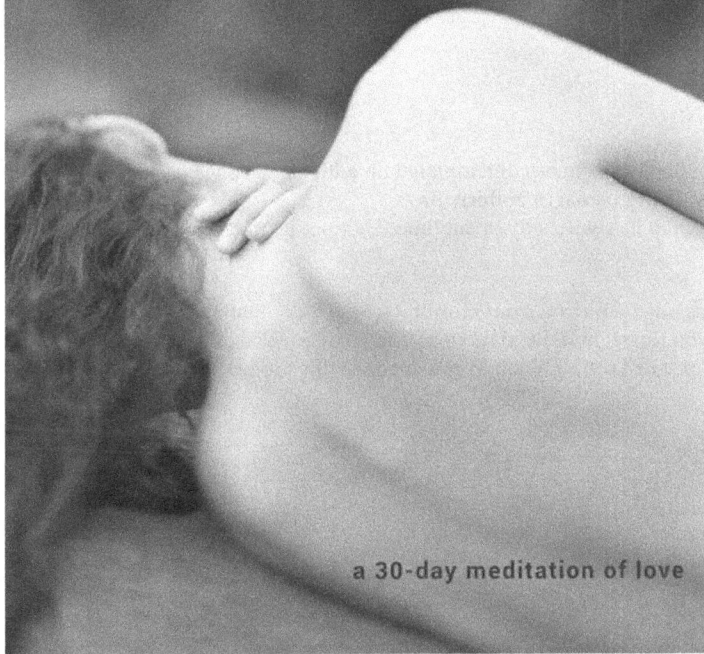

a 30-day meditation of love

By Devi

Copyright © 2018

ISBN:
978-1-7753127-0-3

INTRODUCTION:

This little book of big love is to be contemplated on with one passage each day for thirty consecutive days. Thirty passages in thirty days.
You may find them to be sweet, silly or sublime. They are intended to be all of these, beautiful reader.

Carry the daily passage with you from morning to night, meditating on it every so often as it flows over you throughout the day, or as you are reminded of it due to an experience and/or most certainly when you engage with another.

Blissful,
Devi

March 2018 - Canada

DAY 1
Awaken to love and you will awaken to life.

DAY 2
Linger in love.

DAY 3
Love, in any form, is the highest vibration.

DAY 4
Love deeply, love sweetly, love completely.

DAY 5
Love. Nurture. Repeat.

DAY 6
I'm not here to judge you, I'm here to love you.

DAY 7
Light = Love.

DAY 8
Love is the message and you are the beautiful messenger.

DAY 9
Deeply anything is deeply everything.

DAY 10
The alchemy of love is real.

DAY 11
Think love, speak love, be love.

DAY 12
Pure love is pure truth.

DAY 13
Love yourself MADLY!

DAY 14
Conscious unconditional loving is conscious unconditional living.

DAY 15
Awaken to love.
It is the every thing, the only thing; the ABSOLUTE.

DAY 16
Passion is the fuel for living & loving.

DAY 17
Hearts are never broken, only bruised.

DAY 18

Love clears internal and external pollution.

There is magic in every moment.

DAY 20
Eternity + Infinity = Now.

DAY 21
Even a little love can take you a long way.

DAY 22
Build and beautify your true being.

DAY 23
Ecstasy is everywhere.

DAY 24
Live _to_ love and _for_ love.

DAY 25
The body beckons but the soul summons.

DAY 26
Love is magical never mundane.

DAY 27
In case of emergency: LOVE.

DAY 28
Love creates all things.

DAY 29
LOVE ON!

DAY 30
The Cosmic Tonic is L O V E.

AUTHOR

Devi is a Dakini, Public Speaker, Writer and Teacher.
She embodies deep feminine nurturing and wisdom and has worked professionally with thousands of seekers around the world teaching and touching the way of love.

She has experienced a full Kundalini Awakening and encounters with Extraterrestrial Beings. Devi maintains a private, traditional practice in Canada.
www.divinedakinidevi.com

***

www.ingramcontent.com/pod-product-compliance
Lightning Source LLC
Chambersburg PA
CBHW060551030426
42337CB00019B/3517